A Meditator's Handbook

How to Untie Knots

Bill Crecelius

Vipassana Research Publications

Vipassana Research Publications
an imprint of

Pariyatti Publishing
867 Larmon Road, Onalaska, WA 98570
www.pariyatti.org

Cover design & knot illustrations by
www.danielhaskett.com

Contents

Foreword

We arrived in Bombay around 7 pm after a nice flight from Dubai. Our friends greeted us at the airport to take us to their favorite restaurant. It was a lovely evening. My wife Anne who was not feeling well went to the apartment to rest. The rest of us went on our way. Despite the very heavy traffic it was a mellow evening. After 45 minutes in snarled traffic we were all refreshed and in a pleasant mood when we arrived at the restaurant. There was a huge line outside waiting for tables. It didn't matter what happened—whether it was the heat or the beggars bothering us as we waited—we were completely sanguine despite all inconveniences. The whole evening continued that way.

The next morning I awoke to a similar feeling of good will. I walked into the living room and Anne and our friend were having tea. I sat down and they told me, "Goenkaji passed away last night at 10:40 pm." The *mettā* just started pouring out. I didn't have to do a thing.

We decided to meditate and to go over to his residence to pay our respects. The mellow mood of the previous evening continued, but now accompanied by this *mettā*. When we arrived at the building people had obviously been up since very early that morning getting things ready for a huge crowd of people. As we got there so early, about 10:30 am, there were probably only about 50-60 people. The room was very quiet and people sat in chairs and on cotton carpets on the floor to pay their respects. Everyone seemed very quiet and peaceful. Some were obviously meditating. They were an example of what Goenkaji had taught all his life.

We were taken to an elevator from the large waiting room on the 8th floor up to the 13th floor where Goenkaji and his family lived. He was lying in a glass coffin. This was to be the last time I was to see the man who changed my life. He laid there covered simply in a shawl. We paid our respects and *mettā* just flowed.

We found out from family members that he was in a jovial mood right to the end and his passing was smooth and without incident. He was surrounded by his family at the time.

The reason I have written this book is essentially to help others in some small way as he so greatly did for me. He got me started on the path of Dhamma and inspired me to do so many things I never thought I would do in life. I have not attained to great heights of insight, but I have done what I could because of Goenkaji, and others I came into contact with, while walking on this path. For this I am so thankful.

Acknowledgements

I would like to thank those who helped with editing and inspiration. First to my wife Anne who read through the manuscript many times. Kim Johnston, my old friend from Australia, also helped me and did a fine editing job. When I got the manuscript back and some of the words had been changed to Australian/UK spelling I had to smile, but not quite sure how I was going to change them back.

For many years Robin Curry has been my stalwart whenever I needed anything edited. She would sometimes kick and scream at my request when she thought of the many ways I could mangle the King's English, but she always came through. Needless to say she was there again for me this time. Thanks Robin.

Bharathram Sundararaman a volunteer with Pariyatti who was my official editor and who had many useful suggestions to improve this book. Despite a very busy work and family life, he like so many Dhamma volunteers, took the time to edit this handbook for meditators. Also Brihas Sarathy and Adam Shepard from Pariyatti and Virginia Hamilton. Thanks to Daniel Haskett for creating the cover and knot illustrations.

Thanks also to Rick Crutcher and to Paul and Susan Fleischman for looking over early versions of the manuscript and setting me on a better path.

Introduction

I have learned how to keep my practice together and make it grow. I would like to share this with you. First as a single man living in an area with no other meditators, then living in an area with many other Vipassana meditator friends and finally as a married man with a Dhamma partner, I adapted my life to one of living in the Dhamma.

The path of the monk is high and lofty. It is said that the path for the monk is clear and smooth and easy to walk on. It is high above the muck and mire. There are no stones, pebbles, sharp rocks or thorns. Unfortunately for us poor householders this is not the case. Our lives are bound up in worldly responsibilities, jobs, family ties, and mortgage payments. Unlike the monks, our path is full of worldly impediments and distractions. It is for this reason that I think *A Meditator's Handbook* might help Vipassana students on their walk along this path of purification.

Since you are reading this book, I assume that you have done a course of Vipassana meditation with either Goenkaji or one of his assistant teachers. In the following pages I hope to offer you ways to establish your practice in Vipassana meditation. You may have just recently completed a course, or you may have attended one or more courses some years ago, but couldn't keep up your practice. Either way, this book should be useful to you. Reading this will be more helpful, however, if you decide that you want to make serious efforts to practice this meditation.

When I was young I was a Boy Scout, and I will always remember the Boy Scout Handbook. It had everything you needed to know to be a good scout. As an adult, I became a scout master and came in contact with the handbook again. I realized what a great tool it was for every scout. All the knowledge that was necessary was in that little book.

As I've reflected over the years about working and walking on the path of Dhamma I thought, wouldn't it be great to have a book like this? It wouldn't be about how to tie knots, but how to untie the knots of craving, aversion and ignorance from our minds. This would be a much more practical tool for someone walking on the path of Dhamma.

Luckily, or you could say because of my good karma, I came into contact with many helpful people over the years of my early training. First and foremost was my Dhamma father, Goenkaji, who introduced me to the path of Dhamma and guided me until his death in 2013. Then I was very lucky to meet a number of Sayagyi U Ba Khin's students who had also become teachers. Some lent me a hand on this lifetime project of untying knots. What a great assortment of lessons I learned from them.

In addition I was very fortunate to come in contact with many of Sayagyi's other students, who although they had high attainments were never named as teachers. They also showered me with what they had learned at his feet. Not in any formal way, but by conversation and example over the years.

Of course there were my fellow meditators too. There are so many of these that there is no way to mention them or to even sieve out what lessons they had to share. From some I learned positive things, but from others I learned things by their bad example, as is sometimes the way. I am sorry for them, but thank them nonetheless.

The greatest teacher of all times was the Buddha. He discovered this path that we walk on and instead of keeping it to himself he shared it with all who came to him. Now, all these years later, this lineage of teachers still passes on his actual teaching.

Even over so many centuries and so many generations there were so many people who preserved the teaching, directly and indirectly, for the benefit of future generations! How many teachers were there? We know in the last 100 years or so there have been four (Ledi Sayadaw, Saya Thetgyi, Sayagyi U Ba Khin and Goenkaji), so there probably would have been at least 100 teachers in the lineage spanning the past 2,500 years. Somewhere in that range is the number of *ācariyas* (teachers) that separate us from the Buddha. How fortunate we are that these wonderful, pure hearted people shared this jewel so that we may have it today.

Over these years the teaching has adapted to the times. When the Buddha was alive and for a short time afterwards, there were many *arahants*, fully liberated beings, who kept the teachings ultra pure. As time passed, the lay people supported the monks in more formal ways and what came to be known as the Buddhist religion formed, but it was still almost entirely monks teaching meditation to monks. In our lineage, it was the Venerable Ledi Sayadaw who transmitted the teaching to the farmer Saya Thetgyi who became the first layman teacher. It turned out to be a brilliant move because the 20th century was dawning and a whole new world based on the industrial revolution and computer technology was about to emerge; a new way of transmitting the Dhamma was going to be needed. Saya Thetgyi, Sayagyi U Ba Khin and S.N. Goenkaji did the job he set out for them in amazing style and substance and the world has benefited greatly.

Now we are fortunate to have centers worldwide where people can get the teachings of the Buddha in comfortable, easy to reach locations near most of the major cities of the world. The presentation of the teaching is easy to understand and large numbers of Dhamma workers share their time and *mettā* so more people can get the Dhamma.

May your path be smooth and clear. May you be happy. May you become fully enlightened!

Setting the Record Straight

In a recent conversation with a friend I realized that this book may give the impression that all I do is meditate. Maybe like some kind of quasi-monk. The reality is far from that, although I am very serious about setting aside time to meditate.

Since I started meditating there have been three phases in my life. The first phase was traveling, meditating and immersing myself in Dhamma work. I discovered the path while I was a traveler and during this time much more of my life was devoted to meditation and traveling to India and Burma to do courses and to serve the Dhamma.

Then I got married and we had a son. This started Phase two where I worked at various jobs for the next 27 years and did everything that a normal husband and father does except I included meditation twice a day and usually a 20- or 30- or 45-day course every year. I also totally remodeled a couple of houses, built a few buildings and had many interests including gardening, carpentry, woodworking, Pāli, etc. So I wasn't sitting around watching my navel.

Plus there was all the family stuff like going to soccer games, homework, scouts, camping trips, school projects, etc.

Phase three began when we retired and we started serving the Dhamma full time plus all the above things continued as before.

One does not have to be a recluse to be a meditator. Enjoy the worldly things and maintain your responsibilities, but keep your focus on incorporating the Dhamma into your life. You can do it. The Dhamma will give you the energy to do all you need to do and much more.

Getting Started

You have now experienced the subtleties of the mind and body that are available to you through just one ten-day course in Vipassana meditation.

Although you may have started working at a level that was somewhat superficial when you began, in just ten days you were able to move the mind from a gross level to one that was far subtler. You experienced something else too. By practicing strict rules of morality, you were able to settle the mind so that it would allow you to probe deeper within.

Who would have thought this could happen? Just outside the gates all the chaos and unruly behavior of the everyday world was still going on. But you were living in a cocoon, one that you had chosen to inhabit with the hopes that you would learn something that would help you. Who would have thought that this virtuous lifestyle, combined with a meditation technique that is 2,500 years old, would have given you these feelings of contentment, calmness, joy and compassion for others that you felt at the end of your course.

It may be that it has been some time since you sat a course and those feelings you felt on *mettā* day may not be so prominent in your mind now. If you think about it carefully though, they may return. I remember one day I was driving with a client and he said to me, you know you look really familiar. I said yes you do too. Comparing notes it turned out he did one of the first courses that was held in the United States when Goenkaji came out of India, but he had stopped practicing since then. He said, "You know that was the most profound experience of my entire life." I have heard this many times in the past from people who have sat a course, but had let their practice slip. They still have that experience firmly established in their minds as something so special that it stands out from all the other things they have done since then.

In another case I was having lunch with an old student and she was complaining about not being able to maintain her practice. She had forgotten how deeply beneficial the practice is. The distractions of daily life and old habit patterns interfered. Realizing how superficial her complaints were she said,

"Sometimes I just forget how good practicing is and the benefits I get from it."

Vipassana integrates you into society in a way that is positive, aware, morally sound, and leads to loving other people as much as you love yourself. To gain the wisdom of impermanence (*anicca*) you must exert effort and this will eventually take you to the final goal.

The usual reason people stop sitting after a course is that the strong awareness of the changing nature of sensations (*anicca*) slowly dissipates as one integrates back into society. All of the external stimuli are constantly breaking you down and soon *anicca* is forgotten. Also your morality gets weaker and hence your awareness of *anicca* suffers. If you let this *anicca* slip, you will be facing sittings that are like "yuk." They will be a hard slog all the way through, like the ones at the beginning of a course. If you are not careful, you will let this precious jewel slip away.

When I started practicing, it was as if I had been living with a cloud before my eyes. After taking a course in Vipassana the cloud started to part. There is brightness through those clouds and you can see it. It is similar to when you've been flying at a high altitude and your plane starts to descend through the clouds and it begins to get dark and overcast, but you know on the other side of those clouds is the bright sunlight. Now you have the tool to remove those clouds.

In order to get to that bright sunlight you can make your job easier if you try to live your life by getting rid of distractions that would make it harder for you to walk this Dhamma path. There are various ways to do this and you might find it helpful to your work if you begin now, while the experience of the course is still fresh. However, if you haven't sat a course for a long time, still take this first step, perhaps spending more time on *ānāpāna*. Take another course; this will set you on your way.

During a course at a center, everything is controlled and set up in an orderly way, because meditation is the only activity that takes place there. A lot of thought has gone into the operation of the center based on the experience of many students. It would be helpful for you if a small part of this center experience can be carried over to your ordinary everyday life so there is something that you can grab onto in all the hustle and bustle of being a householder. A place you can touch to remind you of that experience.

Daily Sittings

These two sittings a day are so important. There is no way to emphasize them enough because when you start to miss sittings it becomes harder to meditate. When you first come to a course you may be pretty raw, but by the end of ten days you have seen a transformation in yourself. You are now easily able to feel sensations within, while before the course you probably were totally unaware these sensations even existed. In order to keep a level of Dhammic consciousness within yourself you need this constant sitting. It keeps alive the purity one has established. These two hours a day, morning and evening are absolutely necessary.

You may find it is not as easy to meditate when you return home. You might notice even as you drive away from the center the atmosphere has changed. You are no longer in a place where thousands of people have meditated for many years. Distractions will arise almost at once. When you stop for gas or maybe pick up a newspaper, buy an ice cream or a soft drink there may no longer be any thoughts of the Dhamma. These are all normal things, but you can see the atmosphere of the center can be instantly forgotten. If you are serious about developing a practice you must find a place to be in the spirit of Dhamma that is separate from the mainstream everyday world.

With this in mind the first thing to do is to arrange your sitting place. As Goenkaji mentions in the final discourse of the ten-day course, it is good to have one place to meditate that is always the same. If it is a little bit quiet and away from the usual traffic in the house it will help. A separate room would be ideal. A large closet that isn't being used works very well, even though that's a pretty rare thing, at least in my house. If something this obvious is not available then a place in your bedroom or home office that doesn't get much use will work. A good place is one where you can put your cushions, shawl, timer, etc. and they won't be disturbed. For a list of ideas see Appendix 1.

It is so important to create a space in which you can meditate twice every day. The place will get filled with Dhamma vibrations and feelings of *mettā.* It will become stronger over the years and you will find it easier to meditate there.

You are making an important change in your life. By having a designated meditation place you are creating a habit. This is the place where you come to purify your mind. This is the place where you won't be disturbed so you can walk the path of Dhamma. This place will help you keep on track so you don't forget your sittings. Everything is right there ready to go. It is an instant Dhamma hall.

You may have noticed on day ten, which we call *mettā* day, that once you started talking, everything changed. You were extroverted and thoughts of sitting were gone. At 2:30 pm however there was a sitting. This is a very important sitting and you should reflect on it when you return home and see how hard it can be to meditate. When you began this 2:30 sitting you may have realized immediately that your meditation was different. Your mind was probably distracted or agitated and it was hard to settle down. There may have been aches and pains. Your meditation had changed and you had only been talking a short while. By the end of the hour, however, your mind had probably settled down somewhat and you were pretty much back to where you were at 9 am just before learning the practice of *mettā*. And at 6 pm group sitting you would have seen this happen again.

If you're not careful you won't notice this, but it is a very important lesson. It should give you insight into what is happening in the outside world and why your daily sittings are so important. You will also see that what you are dealing with is natural and it is not that you are doing something wrong. It is easy to think you can't do it or that it is too hard. This actually is a very dangerous situation and one of the most difficult you may face, because you might be tempted to stop sitting when faced with these indistinct or unpleasant sensations or the mind wandering. If you were to stop sitting it would just compound things. It is by sitting that you are able to keep your awareness of the impermanent nature of the sensations and thereby meditate in a proper way. You have to be prepared to accept whatever sensations arise and not have preferences for one or the other. This is equanimity: observing sensations with a balanced mind.

I will give an example. When I returned to the States after my years of travel, I decided to live in Berkeley, California, where I knew there were many other meditators who had also recently returned from India. I knew these friends on the path would support my practice. I rented an apartment and settled down to live a householder's life. One night while I was meditating, it seemed like I had been sitting for at least an hour. I looked at my watch. Ten minutes had passed, nowhere near an hour. I started my practice again and it seemed like another hour had passed. I was so agitated and distracted. I checked my watch again and only five more minutes had passed. This happened a few more times. Fortunately I realized I was at a crossroads; if I let my mind play this trick on me and got up and stopped sitting after only fifteen minutes I would be doomed. That sitting went on and on and on. I thought it would never end. Lifetimes passed, but I did not give up. This never happened again to such a degree. I had overcome this mind that doesn't want to change. This is the kind of thing that you have to guard against as you start your practice at home. The mind will work against you and it won't be the same as it was on the course.

Other hurdles may turn up in your sittings as you begin to practice at home and as you continue from day to day. Sometimes you will find that when you are doing your one-hour sittings you are in a fog. It could be that you even fall asleep during your sittings. This could happen in the morning or the night or possibly both. There is no way to predict when it will happen or even if it will happen. It may seem to you, as it has to others, that you are wasting your time meditating when this happens. I would like to assure you that you are not wasting your time. Even though it may seem that you are trying to walk through mud or swim in molasses it will only pass if you persevere. How do you do this?

21

When this happens and you become aware that you have lost your awareness, start again with as calm a mind as you can muster. Try some *ānāpāna* for a while and some intentional breathing. Make your breath a little stronger so you can feel it. You will rise to the surface of this dull aimless mind from time to time and work with the awareness of sensations and keep knowing their impermanent nature. You will find that it eventually passes. It's possible that there may be only a few minutes in the hour where you are wide awake, sharp, and your mind is penetrating, but these are very valuable minutes. Don't discount them. Use them wisely and don't fret about what you think has been lost. You were working during the entire meditation period, although it might not have been what you expected. If your schedule doesn't demand that you be somewhere right after sitting and at that point your mind is clear, then sit a while longer than an hour. Every moment you sit on the cushion is valuable if you bring your mind back to the object of meditation without reacting. Then you are doing the right thing.

One more thing: there are some people who have exactly the opposite experience. They find that the first ten minutes of the hour they are very sharp, very alert and then they drift into this fog where they don't even know which end is up. It does not matter. Continue to sit, complete the hour. There is no way to know what you are going to experience in your sittings. The object is to make a choiceless observation of whatever sensation presents itself. The same thing applies in all sittings. Observe the sensations that are presenting themselves no matter what you are feeling at that time. Try to lengthen the amount of time you are aware. These gross situations are a manifestation of what is inside you. If you proceed to observe them with equanimity you will be doing your job. If you think about it, after you have been out and about in the world all day dealing with the madness that presents itself, it is not surprising your body feels like a block of cement and it is difficult to feel sensations.

If your mind is not sharp and penetrating, spend more time on *ānāpāna* before switching to Vipassana. A sharp mind will help you to calm down. Likewise a calm mind will make your *samādhi* sharp. When you realize the mind is wandering, try some intentional breathing for a while. If neither of the above works then try meditating with your eyes open for a few minutes and let a little light in.

Whatever you do, don't be defeated, never think all is lost. Just apply right effort to make each sitting successful. They will all be different and when you come to accept this and not expect something you think is "meditating", you will have moved a big step in the right direction.

So once you've established your space you should now discuss this with your family or your roommates. This may be easy for them to accept, but it also may be hard and they could be jealous of this time you take away for yourself. Tell them you have found this meditation practice, which is very important to you. From now on you intend to meditate twice a day, morning and night, one hour each time. This will help you avoid feeling guilty when you have to step away to meditate. Once they know what you are doing they will come to respect you for it, especially when they see positive changes taking place in you.

It is good to try to meditate at the same time every day. You may choose to do it immediately upon arising or just after your morning routine. Maybe you need some energy in the belly first and sit just after you've had your breakfast. Whatever you decide, it is best to keep it the same time every day because that way you will have a routine. If you just leave it to chance you will be lucky if you last a week.

If you live with others it is probably best to meditate before they wake up. That way the house or apartment will be very quiet and you won't be diverted by talking and hanging out. Other people will be a big distraction so be careful. On the other hand if they are meditators too, they can give you strength and you should use their strength to help you. Sit together whenever possible. Try to sit at least one group sitting a day with them.

You should also evaluate your lifestyle. In the evening when you leave work do you stop at the gym on the way home or play a game of tennis or some other sport? When you get home do you usually go for a run or sink into your favorite chair to zone out in front of the TV? Whatever it is you do, think about your evening time. When will it be best to slip in this one hour of meditation? Some people like to sit immediately upon getting home. Others will choose to do it after dinner or before going to bed. You have to make these decisions yourself, but decide what you are going to do as soon as you get home from the course and have set up your meditation sitting place. You have to be skillful. You should have the right intentions. When you prepare like this you will carry them out.

In Berkeley my roommate and I used to sit at 6 am and 6 pm. This worked really well, since many friends knew this and would drop in at those times to join us. Whatever you decide, stick to your plan.

Most importantly you should strive to meditate that first night when you get home from a course. You have just been blasted by such an array of stimuli for the last 8-10, hours since you left the course, you need to get back to where you were when you left the center. By sitting this very first evening, you are building the momentum to establish a pattern that will lead to a strong practice.

A Big Distraction

There is one thing you should consider which is so against the grain of our national culture that I will preface this part with my experience and let you decide for yourself. It may be the black stone in the *kheer* (sweet rice pudding) that Goenkaji talks about in his last discourse, where the child threw away the entire pudding because of a piece of cardamom in the dessert. That big distraction is intoxicants.

When I came out of my first course, I noticed some students threw away their hash and made a commitment to a new way of life, while others would light up a joint. Dope and alcohol are such a part of the Western culture and something that many people don't want to give up at first and more importantly don't see the reason for doing so.

What I discovered during the first few years when I took a drink and then tried to meditate was that it was like a lens that had been smeared with

Vaseline. The dope or the alcohol acts as a filter. In the entertainment business they use a camera lens filter like this, which makes the model or actor that is well past their prime, still look attractive. This is a false impression that is created by using drugs.

Another analogy is when you walk down the street and a shop window has been covered with a white coating while it is being remodeled, so that you can't see in clearly. You can make out some things inside, but everything is fuzzy. This is how drugs and alcohol affect one's perception. They are a mask that doesn't allow one to see what is really happening.

The other mistaken impression is that drugs give one heightened awareness. This is totally false. Some drugs give an altered awareness and some give a modified awareness. It is nothing that will ever help a meditator, because in order to experience the truth, reality must be seen as it is.

Someone who is numbing themselves to drown out some past sorrow may be happy living this way. But relieving past sorrows experienced as sensations is what meditation is about. We have found a tool to deal with the vicissitudes of life, but instead of putting a very sharp edge on that tool to cut through the mess, we dull the tool until it is practically useless.

As a new student you have to make this decision yourself. I was never very good at taking advice from those who were smarter than me until I met Goenkaji. If my father had still been alive when I started meditating he would have probably been shocked that I was listening to someone that was wiser than I was, but he would have also been quite happy.

If you feel you are ready to make such a step at this time—and I hope you will consider it seriously—I have given some guidelines below to help you navigate your task at hand. If not, don't throw the delicious *kheer* pudding away because of a tiny piece of sweet cardamom. Please continue meditation. It is the most important thing.

If you have decided to give it a go, first see what is in the refrigerator or in the cupboard. Is there any alcohol there? Maybe you used to have a glass of wine with dinner or a cold beer on a hot summer day. If any of these things are in there, pour them out. The answer is not to drink them all up to get rid of them and then start afterward. The mind is a slippery thing.

There's one more thing to take care of. Is there a stash somewhere in the house? Any plants growing in the yard? These temptations have to be eliminated or they will pull you down and you will not move forward on the path.

Notice I didn't say give that stuff to a friend. No, don't help someone else fog their mind. This is not your job. You have decided to change your behavior to walk the Path of Dhamma—just because others have not yet made this decision, don't encourage them by giving them intoxicants.

If you do decide at this time to include the fifth precept in your life, there are some occasions where people can become especially pushy while trying to get you to take a drink. These usually are special occasions, such as weddings, New Years, etc. People on these occasions feel there must be a toast. It is a tradition that is very ingrained in the West. There will always be one or two persons who step over the line of good taste and really get in your face to join in the toast with some form of alcoholic beverage. It will be at these times that you must be extremely skillful at standing up for your rights and not be overwhelmed. It is usually handy to have a glass filled with sparkling water or soft drink, and just hold it up and say that you are OK.

Remember you are not alone as you begin to try to live a more Dhammic lifestyle. The power of the Dhamma is very strong. It will help you too.

Dhamma Support

It may seem very difficult to live in a society that doesn't honor people who observe the five precepts, but you will find the forces of nature will come to your aide. For instance one of the aides will be your daily sitting. When you sit in a designated place each time, the place you chose will begin to be charged with vibrations of Dhamma. Even though it will only be very small at first, this will grow. Then when you sit down to meditate you will know you are entering a Dhammic place, even if it is only three feet by three feet.

To help this place get stronger more quickly begin to invite your friends over who are also meditators in this tradition. Have a group sitting with them at your sitting place. They can gather around you as you all sit together. All of you will be benefiting. Maybe invite them for dinner and socialize with them. You will find all those *sīla* (morality) concerns are no longer concerns with these friends. It will be easier to live a life of Dhamma.

Another helpful thing to do would be to get copies of Goenkaji's chantings. When you play them in your meditation area these words of Dhamma chanted over and over again will assist you. The evening discourses are also available. Every time you hear them you will learn something new.

The next thing to know about is group sittings. These are activities you should strive to attend. Sitting with others who practice this technique will recharge your batteries. It will be almost as good as sitting at a center. These sittings are published on the web site of your local center or you can ask about group sittings where you sat your last course. These aren't social events, but a chance to practice with like-minded people so you can all build your practice together. You will all benefit from this boost. If there isn't one near you and you know someone else in your area who sits Vipassana as taught by S.N. Goenka, get together with them, choose a time and place, and sit regularly, weekly if possible. You will get strength from group sittings.

One-day sittings are another helpful support for your practice. You can look online to see if you live in an area where there are one-day sittings. By attending a one-day sitting you can strengthen your awareness of the impermanent nature of the sensations (*anicca*) you are feeling and this will help you to have better and stronger sittings. One third of the time you will be doing *ānāpāna* and two thirds of the time you will practice Vipassana. By the end of the day your *anicca* level might even be back up to where it was when you left your last course. This is so important if you want to maintain a daily practice.

If there aren't any one-day sittings in your area and if there is an Assistant Teacher that lives nearby perhaps if you ask, he/she can help you to arrange them from time to time. The other meditators in your area will thank you. If this is not the case, then you can do them regularly yourself. For the first two years after I returned from India, I sat a one-day self course every other weekend. This gave me a lot of strength and it will do the same for you. The best is to start at 4:30 a.m. and work through till 9:00 pm, which is what I did, but even if you don't do that you will find if you just use the relaxed schedule they use at the official one day sittings—9:00 am to 4:00 or 5:00 pm—they will be a big help.

If convenient, you can also go to the center for a group sitting, special Dhamma service period, short course, or other event.

The thing that you have to remember about one-day sittings and group sittings is they help you to tune up your practice. The sights, sounds and images that we are blasted with all day pull us down. Maybe you aren't very aware of it, maybe you are, but it is pretty much hate, greed and delusion all day. Professionals have become experts at diverting our minds; universities teach classes in how to get peoples' attention, in conscious and even unconscious ways, to be able to influence them. Buy this, lust after that, over and over it plays out continuously. When they leave the monastery, monks go around with their heads down and do not divert their eyes, in order to avoid all this stimuli. You will be able to eliminate some of it by what you choose to read and watch on television and what movies you see, but even then it permeates the air. It also fills the web sites we visit, our email and now even our telephones. So these one-day sittings will be so important in refocusing your mind on the nature of impermanence. When you sit on the cushion it is as if you pour yourself through a strainer; you go through, but all the junk stays in the strainer. You arise from your cushion refreshed.

On day eleven Goenkaji gives the instruction that students should try to do one ten-day course a year. If you follow this advice it will be a huge benefit. During that one course per year you will be able to deepen your practice.

Imagine that you have dug a small trench. During the year the trench keeps getting dirt and dust knocked into it. By the end of the year it is full or nearly full. In the same vein if you were not cleaned out by your daily practice, group sittings, one-day courses and three-day courses you would become full and you would have to start over again. To stop this from happening you have to keep cleaning out the ditch. If you then take another course you will be able to deepen that trench. With less dirt and dust to remove, your work on the ten-day retreat will progress much faster with fewer hindrances. Of course if your *sīla* (morality) has not been good it will make it much more difficult. But if you are striving for good *sīla*, you will be in good shape to make quicker and deeper progress in your annual course.

There will be some people who find they have more time to practice meditation than just two hours a day and one ten-day course a year. If this is your case there is nothing wrong with doing more than one course per year. Many students find that they really want to set a strong foundation and they decide to go to a center in order to sit and serve over a period of time. By doing this, you will have a friendly place to establish your practice and deepen it. You will be able to apply what you have learned while living in the protected environs of the Dhamma center. And when you later return to your life in the outside world, you will take with you the strong and solid habit of sitting regularly and experiencing *anicca*. Thus you will be able to continue your practice with greater ease.

In fact I have seen a direct correlation between those that do Dhamma service and those that have a strong practice. The practice contributes to the service and vice versa.

The Buddha said there is no more fertile field than a person practicing meditation, so it is very beneficial to serve these students. When you help to serve those who have the ability to grow strong in meditation, you are helping them as well as yourself.

Dhamma Friends

W hen I returned from India I moved to the San Francisco Bay area because I knew there were other meditators there who I had known in India. When I returned to the States the area where my family lived was a desert, in terms of other meditators, so I went where I knew there were meditators. The second day I moved to Berkeley I attended a group sitting, and I met people who I still associate with today.

For approximately 20 years after that, I rarely missed a weekly group sitting. This helped me tremendously. Most of the people I met at those sittings were the ones that helped to get the Dhamma established in North America and in California in particular. It has been a rich way of life because of these associations and because of these group sittings.

In my case, moving to a town where I knew few people other than meditators made it easy for me. Almost all my friends were other meditators. I wasn't pulled in many different directions by all of my acquaintances. We went to the movies together, played sports together, ate out together and so forth. This made it easier to progress. Most people who come to the Dhamma will have a different experience. It will be beneficial to make some friends who are Vipassana meditators and can be a Dhamma touch stone. Slowly, as one of the qualities of the Dhamma, *ehi passiko* (come and see), manifests itself, even members of your family and other friends may come to the Dhamma. As years go by you will find fellow meditators become a great support for your practice.

Developing Dhamma friends will make you strong in the Dhamma, which means you will have a happier life. The Buddha actually considered this one of the most important parts of the path of Dhamma. This is what the Buddha said to Ānanda when he approached the Buddha to discuss this.

On one occasion the Buddha was living among the Sakyans at a town named Sakkara. Ānanda, on returning from his morning alms round in the town, approached the Buddha. He greeted him and sat to one side. He addressed the Buddha and said that during his alms round he had been thinking and that it came to him the importance of friends, while living the holy life. He said, "Bhante, half of the holy life is having virtuous people as friends, companions and colleagues."

The Buddha replied, "Don't say that Ānanda. Don't say that. Having virtuous people as friends, companions and colleagues is actually the whole of the holy life. When a bhikkhu has virtuous people as friends, companions and colleagues, it can be expected that he will pursue the Noble Eightfold Path and that he will develop in it."

I have found this advice of the Buddha's to be influential in my life. These *kalyāna mittā* (friends in Dhamma) have helped me on the path. They have guided me on the path. They have not tried to misguide me.

Foolish people have brought down more meditators than any other power on earth.

The words, "Don't associate with fools," are probably the most important words the Buddha ever spoke to a householder who is new to the path of Dhamma. This may apply to the not-so-new student as well. These words are the very first line of the *Maṅgala Sutta*, a *sutta* wherein the Enlightened One explained the highest welfares that a meditator has. The Buddha thought that it was so important that he started the *sutta* (discourse) with this warning:

Asevanā ca bālānaṃ,
paṇḍitānañca sevanā;
pūjā ca pūjanīyānaṃ,
etaṃ maṅgalamuttamaṃ.

Avoidance of fools,
the company of the wise;
honor where honor is due,
this is the highest welfare.

Making Choices

After one leaves the center having just completed a meditation course, one has many choices. What am I going to do? Where am I going to go? One of the choices people will not consciously consider is probably, will I associate with fools?

Unfortunately some of the people we know behave in foolish ways that might hurt them and may hurt us too. They are people who don't lead their lives through skillful action. What is skillful action? Skillful action is developing one's strengths and virtues by living in accordance with the Eightfold Path of the Buddha's teaching and in this case we are talking primarily about *sīla* (morality).

Of course we can't entirely stop associating with people who are foolish or don't have good moral behavior. Even householder meditators with the best of intentions aren't able to keep perfect *sīla* (morality), but there are degrees and that is something you might like to consider at this point.

It has been my experience there are people who have a low level of morality. Sometimes we can't avoid them. It will help you if, at the very least, you are wary and watchful around them. We cannot abandon them, and should still have *mettā* for them.

You may have heard from someone that morality is not important. There were those that had similar views during the time of the Buddha. He clearly explained that this type of thinking was harmful and should be avoided. Today it might be called the school of, "if it feels good, do it." But this school is not correct, at least not for someone who is thinking of walking a very long path of purity in action. The person that says morality is not important is a foolish person. They are giving bad advice. It seems that people who feel this way usually like to lead others down the path they are taking, but the path of Dhamma diverges from any path like this quite sharply.

When you started your course you were asked to take five precepts. It was one of the opening formalities. Now that the course is over you have been freed from those formalities but the practice of *sīla,* morality, is still the foundation of the practice. In order to progress on the path it will help you a lot if you take those five precepts to heart. There will be no one asking you to do this, there will be no one watching over you to make sure you are doing it. If you would like to begin practicing a Dhamma way of life this is the first step. When you go on a hike you have to make sure you are prepared. You need your walking shoes, a bottle of water, maybe some sunscreen and a power bar in case you get hungry. No one tells you this is what you will need, it is just common sense. To walk on this path, what you will need is *sīla, samādhi* and *paññā*. These are the basics for your hike on this new path.

Consider this; when do you think you should start to behave in a proper way, a moral way? Is there some point after which you give up breaking *sīla* and then all of a sudden you just start behaving skillfully? The answer is that it must be inculcated from the beginning. If you don't start right away, all that time you will be building more and more *saṅkhāras* (mental reactions) and more *dukkha* (suffering). This does not help your progress.

Breaking *sīla* pulls you down. It preoccupies your mind with worry and concern. Will I be found out? What will happen if people learn of this action that I took? The balanced mind that is required for deep meditation will be less accessible to you. It also hurts other people. If you steal, then someone has had a loss. You've had a gain, but at a very high price. And so it goes with all the five *sīlas*. There will be no peace of mind for you.

Perfect *sīla* is only possible for an *arahant* (a fully liberated being), but for a student on the path if one is trying to earnestly keep his *sīla*, that effort will be good enough. You should try to keep your *sīla* and work with right effort toward that goal. You may slip from time to time, but consider, did you slip because you were overwhelmed by craving or aversion and reacted blindly? Or did you slip because you just decided to let it go this one time? There is a difference. If you are overwhelmed you will recover, but if you decide to just let it go this time you will find that it will turn into another time, and another. You will be defeated. So do your best, this is the middle path.

Just Keep Knowing *Anicca*

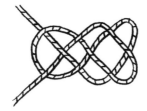

If someone were to count the number of times that Goenkaji mentions *anicca* (change, imperma-nence) during a course they would be amazed. He says it over and over. He is trying to drive home a point, but many students just gloss over it, or miss it entirely. He repeats it because it is IMPORTANT.

One of the most important things to remember as a new student or even a student that has done dozens of courses is *anicca*. Goenkaji continually remarks, "maintain equanimity and keep knowing *anicca*" or "maintain equanimity with the appreciation of *anicca*." He ends the instructions at the beginning of each sitting with these words after Vipassana is introduced. What does he mean when he says this? Why do you think he keeps saying it over and over?

Keep knowing *anicca* means to be aware of the sensations you are feeling and know that they are changing and impermanent and to continue doing this for as long as you can. When you realize you have stopped observing this object then begin again.

Every moment as you pass your attention through your body, whether going part by part or when you are working with the flow, in order to get the full benefit of your efforts, you have to continually be aware that these sensations are changing. There is never a moment when they are not changing. Most likely until you started practicing Vipassana you were never aware of it, or maybe vaguely aware intellectually but were not experiencing it. Now you are aware of the sensations, but that is not enough, you must also be aware and try to experience that within that sensation there is an oscillation that is changing. It is *anicca*. It doesn't matter if the sensation is so subtle that you can barely experience the arising and falling within the sensation you are feeling. It doesn't matter if it is gross pain or a dull area. Just be aware that as your attention reaches this spot that it is changing.

The entire universe is changing; you are changing. Everything is *anicca*. It is the knowledge that one must have, as well as *dukkha* (suffering) and *anattā* (insubstantiality), to attain *nibbāna*. The Buddha said, "If one knows *anicca* then one knows *dukkha* and *anattā*". In order to make this a part of you, you will need to inculcate this state of reality into your mind.

In his book *Satipaṭṭhāna*, the Venerable Anālayo says, "Continuity in developing awareness of impermanence is essential if it is really to affect one's mental condition. Sustained contemplation of impermanence leads to a shift in one's normal way of experiencing reality, which hitherto tacitly assumed the temporal stability of the perceiver and the perceived objects. Once both are experienced as changing processes, all notions of stable existence and substantiality vanish, thereby radically reshaping one's paradigm of experience."

Part of the problem is that the awareness of *anicca* is difficult to implement in your practice. Another part of the problem is that one doesn't hear what Goenkaji is saying or doesn't feel it is important. Students are consumed by just trying to feel sensation. You have felt sensation and you are also aware that it is not important what type of sensation you feel. Any sensation is good. Gross or subtle, it doesn't matter. Now remember that this sensation is changing. It is *anicca*. That's all there is to it. Feel the sensation while also being equanimously aware of its arising and passing. It is simple, but not easy to do.

At first you may keep forgetting that your goal is not only to be aware (*sati*) of the sensations (*vedanā*) but also to let a part of your mind be aware that these sensations are changing. This awareness will slip away, but as soon as you realize that you have forgotten then start knowing *anicca* again. Of course it will again slip away. This is a training. A training of the mind, so when you realize it again start to be aware of the fact that the sensation you are feeling is impermanent.

Just think about this: When your teacher kept mentioning something over and over again in class, didn't you get it that this was going to be on the exam? When your teacher in college said, "You might see this again." Wasn't that a signal that it was going to be on the test? Well the test you are taking is called Life and the answer to the Vipassana quiz is "Just keep knowing *anicca*." If you know that answer you can't fail the test. Not only that, but your life will be successful.

Within the sensations there is this arising and falling. It may be happening slowly. Arising … falling. Or it may be happening very, very quickly. Just observe that. Be aware of that. It doesn't matter if it is hot or cold, itchy or painful, vibrating or dull. Just be aware of that arising and falling, *anicca*. That should be your goal. That is all you have to do; feel the sensation and know its impermanent nature. Continually feel it without interruption and don't react. If you have any questions about this or other aspects of your practice, please contact the Vipassana center where you took your most recent course and request that an Assistant

Teacher contact you. You can find Vipassana center contact information at *www.dhamma.org*.

Slowly it will become a part of your practice. The first step is to try. You won't have to worry because Goenkaji's chanting will constantly be reminding you:

Aniccā vata saṅkhārā...

Impermanent, truly, are compounded things...

Bingo Bango *Bhaṅga*

O ne of the biggest traps students fall into is the craving for subtle sensations. The mind naturally tends towards craving for pleasant sensations and aversion to unpleasant sensations. This is its conditioning. This is the cause of suffering. The training is to come out of suffering. Very soon after starting Vipassana, Goenkaji begins telling students to observe things as they are. He says that whatever sensation comes up you are to just observe that. Instead many students want something they don't have and begin craving.

On day nine of the ten-day course he discusses *bhaṅga* for the first time. *Bhaṅga* is when your body opens up and the entire mass is filled with very subtle sensations. For this to take place you don't have to do anything, it just happens. The word has such a ring to it that it sometimes creates confusion in students' minds. It just rings with the sound of something special. We think, "Oh, this must be important, I must get this. This is what I want."

Ah, that is what you *want*. It isn't what *is*, but it is what you *want*. This becomes a problem for you because as you know, as soon as you start craving you are running in the opposite direction of the Dhamma. You are not being equanimous, you are reacting.

It is best to understand what *bhanga* is. It is a natural phenomenon that may occur in meditation. Almost all of the sensations that manifest themselves on your body while you are meditating are just the past conditionings of your mind expressed on your body. Other causes may be the food that you eat, the atmosphere around you, or your present thoughts. You have no control over these sensations because you can't make them. You actually made them in the past and now because your mind is quiet and non-reacting they are appearing on and sometimes in the body. It is nature unfolding itself.

When one starts Vipassana, many times one feels gross, solidified sensations. As the hours and days pass, as one reaches greater depths of awareness, one notices more subtle sensations appear in different areas of the body. It may be that there are subtle sensations everywhere on the surface of the body. When this happens we call it free flow and you can easily move your attention in a sweeping movement along the surface of the body. When those sensations penetrate throughout the body, inside and outside, and there are no blockages, this is *bhaṅga*. Blockages are areas that are blind, blank, misty, cloudy, or dense.

The sensations associated with *bhaṅga* are very pleasurable. Because of this, many students think this is the goal of meditation. However, this is not the case. The sensations are constantly changing. One moment there may be pain, the next there may be heat or cold, etc., and the next there may be a pleasurable sensation. The trouble arises when the student likes that pleasurable sensation but, like the previous sensations, these also change, *anicca, anicca*. Yet, you *want* that sensation. Then the game of sensations begins. It is a game that can't be won.

Sometimes years pass and students keep up the sensation game. They kid themselves and they kid the teacher. Thinking they are making progress on the path, but they are stuck. Possibly they don't believe what the teacher is saying or they think everyone has subtle sensation and they are the only one that doesn't. Or they get hung up thinking this is the goal they are searching for. Course after course they chase after subtle sensations. You must keep in mind that this is not the goal you are working toward. When you reach the goal there will be no sensations.

Imagine that you are traveling on a train and some beautiful view appears outside the window. As the train moves you think I must keep that view in sight and you start running through the train. After knocking over women and children and tripping over luggage, conductors and all manner of things you will reach the back of the train and still that view will disappear. If you saw someone doing this you would think they were crazy. Yet, many people do exactly the same thing trying to hold onto some sensation.

You have no control over when *bhaṅga* will come or go. It is the same with all sensations. You have no control over them. They arise because of the types of *saṅkhāras* manifesting on the body or because of the present thoughts or because of the atmosphere or the food that one eats. As a meditator, you have only one job and that is to watch the sensations as they arise and keep knowing *anicca*. Taking the example of the train, it would be as if you were looking at the window watching the scenery go by. You would neither like it or not like it, you would just watch it. When you do this, all the benefits that derive from this meditation will come to you. If you head in the opposite direction you are just wasting your time and creating more suffering for yourself.

Since you cannot change the sensations, the sooner you decide to accept them, be equanimous with them and not react, the sooner you will begin making progress on the path. By deciding otherwise, you are automatically choosing *dukkha* (suffering).

The *Pāramī* Paradox

An unusual situation must be overcome in order to progress on the path of Dhamma. In order to attain full enlightenment there are ten mental qualities that must be developed. They are known as *pāramitās* or *pāramīs*, which means perfections that must be fulfilled.

These *pāramīs* when developed give us the strength to progress on the path of wisdom. When the *pāramīs* are weak one's practice is also weak. Having a strong practice makes it easier to develop these *pāramīs* but if you don't have them you will have trouble progressing on the path. So how do you get strong *pāramīs*? This is the paradox.

These ten *pāramīs* are:

Generosity (*Dāna*)

Morality (*Sīla*)

Renunciation (*Nekkhamma*)

Wisdom (*Paññā*)

Effort (*Viriya*)

Tolerance (*Khanti*)

Truthfulness (*Sacca*)

Strong Determination (*Adhiṭṭhāna*)

Selfless Love (*Mettā*)

Equanimity (*Upekkhā*)

If you review this list you will see that someone with these qualities has good morality, a balanced mind, and the ability to work despite hardships that must be overcome when one meditates in their daily life. They are the perfections that a fully liberated being (*arahant*) achieves to attain the final goal. You must also eventually have possession of all of these *pāramīs,* and in sufficient quantities too, before you can become fully liberated. In fact you already possess quite abundant *pāramīs*. If you didn't, you would not have had the curiosity to take even one step on the path. When you heard the words "Vipassana", "Goenka", "insight", you would not have had the slightest interest or inclination to proceed. You would not have wanted to find out more. Reflect on the *pāramīs* and you will see the direction you need to proceed.

You need to be aware of the *pāramī* paradox so that when an opportunity arises to develop one of the *pāramīs* you take the initiative. This needs to be done both in everyday life and on courses. By being aware, you will strengthen your practice and become a happier person and a better meditator.

Recently I heard the story of a student who upon completing his first course began showing up between courses to help clean up the center after the just completed course and then helped in setting up for the next course. He came at every interval. He worked from early in the morning till late at night. He was in his late sixties and had retired recently from a corporate job. Some people became concerned that he might burn out working so hard. When an Assistant Teacher talked with him to see how he was doing, he said, "You guys all started when you were young and have had many years building up your *pāramīs*. I've just started and I have a lot of catching up to do, that is why I try to serve as much as possible." Now that is a person who has a very good understanding of the *pāramī* paradox and isn't going to let anything stand in his way to reach the final goal.

One opportunity to develop the *dāna* (generosity) perfection is on day ten of a course. When the sign up sheet comes around for chores that are needed to clean up the center, this is your opportunity to help others.

A few times a year an announcement is sent about a work weekend, work period or possibly a shortage of servers for the next course. Now, with this understanding of the *pāramī* paradox, it would be helpful to think, "Ah, this is an opportunity for me to build my *dāna pāramī.*"

You may have a very busy job or a lot of family commitments that might preclude you from giving service. At times like these in life it might be easier for you to give actual money rather than service. This helps to dissolve your ego. In this way you share the benefits you have received to help others. Many individuals have given everything that you see at a center. From the land to the light bulbs, some student has donated towards it. Due to the policy of centers in this tradition of only taking voluntary donations from those who have completed a ten-day course, the development of a center is a slow process.

A good example is the center in Massachusetts, the first center to arise in North America. A house with a few acres was purchased by a handful of students in 1982. At first, everyone was crammed into the house for courses and the Dhamma hall was so small people were sitting knee-to-knee and happy to get a seat. Every nook and cranny was used for something, even the basement, which was a makeshift dining hall. During the summer, tents allowed additional students to join courses and at first a big tent was used for a larger Dhamma hall. And now, in

2015, there is a large complex of buildings serving many students every year. Most of the rooms have private baths and there is a pagoda with individual cells for meditation. In this way, slowly, all the centers have come up. The centers have been built one step at a time in a practical, financially conservative manner. Now there are fifteen centers in North America (that includes Mexico, the U.S. and Canada) with two more where land has been purchased, but buildings have yet to be built.

Consider the other benefits that will come into play if you go to the center for a Dhamma service weekend. You will be sitting three times a day. You will be making the center a stronger and better place for others to come to. It is an opportunity to build your practice. This is an excellent opportunity if you want to overcome this *pāramī* paradox. You will overcome it only with your effort (*viriya*), which is itself another *pāramī*.

Should you decide to join a work weekend you will have an opportunity to practice the *nekkhamma pāramī*. You will also be renouncing the world (*nekkhamma*) for two days like you do when you take a course. You will live off the donations of others. You will practice the middle path without extremes, living a very wholesome lifestyle. In traditional Buddhist countries for 2,500 years lay people have been setting aside certain days each month called *uposatha* days where they practice the *pāramīs* with more strenuous effort. They take eight or even ten precepts for those days. Some of them practice meditation too.

Tolerance (*khanti*) is a quality that when found in others is highly appreciated. These are people who don't criticize, condemn or complain. People who have tolerance are usually liked by others and easy to get along with.

A meditation course offers many opportunities to practice tolerance. Is your neighbor meditator quiet or noisy? Do they move around a lot? Maybe they breathe heavily. Perhaps the food has some missing ingredient or was accidentally burnt that morning by the volunteer staff. If your reaction to these situations is accepting and non-judgmental you will be increasing your *pāramī* of tolerance.

Every day we are faced with opportunities to strengthen this quality in ourselves as we go through our life. Especially in today's world where people are encouraged to be assertive, assertiveness and intolerance can easily get mixed up. If you have to wait in line, spend the time feeling the changing nature of the sensations within yourself instead of fretting or getting agitated. Traffic jams are an excellent place to practice awareness of change and to be tolerant. Intolerance comes mostly when we feel someone else is personally affronting us. Most likely they are unaware of this affront. Anger and hatred are usually the result, which work against our efforts to walk on the path and we simply build up more and more *saṅkhāras* (mental reactions).

Strong determination (*adhiṭṭhāna*). During a course do you take this seriously? It is important because as your practice progresses there will be challenges that will require this *pāramī* be developed to a high degree, or else you will easily become defeated. You must be able to carry out any intention you have. On a course you are told to observe and not to react. For one hour this is your goal. The reason for this is we are constantly reacting in life to every situation. If you can change that habit pattern you will see that you soon stop reacting blindly as you go through daily life. On a course, during the one-hour vows (*adhiṭṭhāna*) we get to practice this three times a day. The path of Dhamma is a path that takes determination. If you build on it each step of the way you will find it there when you need it.

Do you complete every task you start out to do or do you start things and never finish them? Outside the course you can also develop the *pāramī* by finishing those things you start. This will build up your *pāramī* of *adhiṭṭhāna*.

Equanimity (*upekkhā*). Some people have

trouble understanding this word. "Equanimity" or "equanimous" means to be balanced and not to react. We need a balanced mind to progress on the path. If we are shaken by the slightest obstacle or agitated easily we must find a way to bring our minds back to a place where we can observe equanimously. Some students find their problem is that they get thrown off the track by trying too hard. They are gritting their teeth, thinking I've got to get this and thinking that by pushing harder it will help. It won't. It takes balance not strength. Many students on courses have received much benefit from just taking a walk for five minutes rather than trying to push through their pain or agitation. The stories of monks breaking their knee bones and not moving until they are fully liberated are of people whose *pāramīs* are fulfilled and not of ones that are just starting on the path.

In Burma at Kyaiktiyo, the Golden Rock, there is a huge boulder that is balanced on just a very small spot. The entire weight of that boulder plus the pagoda that has been built on top of it, is balanced on just a very small area. The boulder is unshakable. If your equanimity was focused like the weight of that rock you would be unshakeable too.

Morality (*sīla*). There is less chance of you breaking your *sīla* while staying at a center. Of course *sīla* is something that you can work on whether at a center or not. Remember those five *sīlas* and apply them all the time. The really gross ones like not killing and not stealing take a fair amount of effort to break. For someone who has sat a course or a few courses you have to make some effort to get in trouble with these. Hopefully, you have used your increased awareness and your understanding of the Buddha's teachings to move past these. But, there is one that you have to really watch out for and that is right speech. Oh, this is such a pit to fall into. So easily, so quickly, our mouth opens and we have broken this *sīla*. It happens every day and so fast. The words are out and we've done it again. The Buddha was particularly contemptible of lying. This is what he had to say.

The Consequences of Wrong Speech

This was said by the Bhagavā [the Buddha], this was said by the Arahat and heard by me. "That person, O Bhikkhus, who transgresses this one thing, there is, I dare say no evil deed whatsoever he would not perform. What is this one thing?

This, O Bhikkhus, is telling a lie consciously."

—Musāvādasuttaṃ from *Saṃyutta Nikāya, Mahāvagga,* Translated by Klaus Nothnagel

Don't let yourself fall in this trap or any of the other forms of wrong speech such as slander, backbiting, gossip, harsh words or setting one against another.

Effort (*viriya*) should be made to keep those good qualities you already have and try to increase these qualities. Try to eliminate the bad qualities you have and be sure not to add any more. This is the essence of *viriya*.

In addition there is a certain level of industriousness needed to make this long trek to the final goal. There is the effort of getting started, the effort of continuing, expending effort from moment to moment without sliding backwards. The moment that effort is dropped the mind begins to wander or you fall asleep. Too much effort on the other hand is another problem because you will then experience tension. Effort is a balancing act. Say that you caught a butterfly. If you held onto the butterfly too tightly you would crush it, if you didn't hold onto it with enough effort it would fly away. In the middle is the balance.

Sayagyi U Ba Khin is quoted as saying that you must be as soft as a flower and as hard as a stone. Effort (*viriya*) is a very important *pāramī*.

You are involved in a training. You are training to be a better person and eventually an *arahant*. It is a long training, very long, but you have already started so all you have to do is work to get better at the task at hand.

Mettā and You

How can something you can't see but only feel help you and benefit all beings? The power of *mettā* will only become known to you when you use it and experience it. Every day at the end of your sittings it is wise to practice *mettā* for a few minutes. This means filling the bodily sensations you are feeling with thoughts of loving kindness toward all beings, also towards beings that are near and dear to you. This could be your partner, your children, your friends or other family members. They are a good place to start because you already have good feelings towards them. Sometimes in the hustle and bustle of the day we drop our awareness and may say or do something that might upset our loved ones or acquaintances. It may be that this situation may have happened in the distant past or just today, but practicing *mettā* with these people in mind can produce amazing results.

I have seen this in my own life and those of my friends. I've seen where troubled relations between husbands and wives have been healed or where relations with other family members that were distant or non-existent were soon made whole again. There is no underestimating this power of *mettā*.

Also it is not only for use within your own family, but also with co-workers and those outside. Mrs. Jocelyn King, one of Sayagyi U Ba Khin's students, tells the story of Sayagyi U Ba Khin's situation: "Sayagyi had been asked to be a member of a certain government committee. The other members were very hostile to him when he first joined the group. Over time he completely turned this situation around". When Mrs. King asked him how he did it, he said, "with *mettā.*"

In this world with all its negative forces, someone who has *mettā* within becomes a force for good and those around will know this. Goenkaji would never have been able to do the tremendous job he has done of spreading the Dhamma around the world in such a short time if it hadn't been for the strong *mettā* vibrations that surrounded him all the time. Where there is light, darkness cannot come.

One time in San Francisco we were to have a meeting with the Northern California Trust and Goenkaji. The meeting was to be held in a hotel room that had been used previously by an airline crew on a stop over. The environment felt harsh and non-dhammic. Goenkaji's room in the same hotel, on the other hand, felt wonderful. We suggested maybe the meeting should be held there instead. Goenkaji's secretary, Yadav, said, "Don't worry it will be fine." As we rode the elevator up to the floor where the meeting was to be held the whole elevator buzzed with the vibrations of *mettā*. As we entered the room the whole room buzzed with the vibrations of *mettā*. *Mettā* did it all.

Please don't just share *mettā* with those you know. There are so many beings everywhere that are suffering. It is part of being born. When you practice *mettā*, be sure to share with all beings whether you see them or not and whether you know them or not. The forces of good in the world can only grow if more people practice *mettā*.

The chanting that Goenkaji does every morning fills the center with vibrations of *mettā*. Over the years this builds and builds. When people step into a center they say it is so peaceful here. Yes, that's true, it is peaceful. It is the *mettā* they are feeling.

You may have noticed the wild animals at the center where you took your course. In the Massachusetts center there are many rabbits. There is hardly any animal as skittish as a rabbit, yet these rabbits live in the atmosphere of Dhamma and *mettā*. If you are on the walking path and walk by them they just sit there eating their grass as if you didn't exist. In Australia it is the same with the kangaroos, which are usually very wild and skittish animals. Even the little Joeys barely look at you as you walk past. This shows the result of people practicing *mettā* and not harming other beings.

By regularly practicing meditation in your home, the room you use for sittings will also become a place where people come and say "Oh, it is so peaceful here." They will like it and not even know what it is.

What One Can Learn from Books

There are many interesting books written on the teachings of the Buddha. The amount is vast. Some of it is good and some of it bad, like most things. Pariyatti (*www.pariyatti.org*) was started by a meditator and it has a large inventory of books that relate to this tradition. They are also the North American distributors for the Buddhist Publication Society (BPS) of Sri Lanka, the Pali Text Society (PTS) of England, and carry many books from the Vipassana Research Institute (VRI) of India.

I have obtained a lot of pleasure out of books about the Dhamma and it helped me understand some of the concepts discussed in the discourses. For quite a few years, I would read every evening before going to bed. Setting a regular time aside like that was very helpful in developing a reading program in a busy life. I have included a reading list in Appendix 2.

Pariyatti (studying the Dhamma from books) can be a great inspiration to meditators. Words of Dhamma are sweet and can give us great inspiration to work deeper in our practice. Reading of the times of the Buddha and his teachings can give us a push in the right direction, but pick a time that is not intended for your practice of meditation to do this. The *suttas* (discourses) are wonderful, Pāli has a lovely sound to it and is used in many of Goenka-ji's discourses, so it is important to learn at least the basic terms that you hear again and again, but when you hit a rough spot in your practice don't try substituting reading and study for actual practice. A rough spot can be when you can't sit for an hour because you find it hard or there is always something more important to do. Maybe you start finding excuses to not sit. It is a slippery slope if you stop practicing and start studying. You will end up not doing the most important thing you have ever learned.

Keep these two things separate. One is *suta-mayā paññā* (something you have heard) and the other is *bhāvanā-mayā paññā* (what you have experienced). This is a path of experience. One may read and study for eons and yet never move even one inch on the path of Dhamma. Webu Sayadaw, who gave Sayagyi U Ba Khin and all who met him, tremendous inspiration, was considered by many to be an *arahant*. He realized very early in his monkhood, that in order to attain the final goal he must leave the teaching monastery, where they only taught learning the *suttas*, and go to the jungle to practice Vipassana. He realized that studying the texts would not help him attain full liberation. His goal was full liberation, not intellectual understanding. His decision proved correct for him and it will for you. Webu Sayadaw realized that solely book learning was a dead end for someone with the *pāramīs* to be a meditator and so must you.

Summing Up

Like a scoutmaster who guides his scouts to become successful using the techniques in the Scout Handbook, I hope that some of this will help you to be better at untying the knots of hate, greed and delusion that make up so much of our being. It is by steady and correct practice that this success will come about. It cannot be assimilated by being near a person who has attained higher levels of development. It cannot be attained by reading books, listening to discourses or chanting. It cannot be handed down from parent to child. Success can only come about by practice. The result will be commensurate with the amount of balanced effort expended.

The Scout Handbook actually helps young scouts to have a really great time when they are in the outdoors. They learn how to do things correctly and easily so they won't get hurt or harmed. Hopefully this handbook will make your life peaceful and full of joy. When you start seeing things as they really are, you won't be dragged down by the negative, and you will become brighter and lighter. That's what it's all about isn't it? When the darkness goes, there is only the light left.

If you don't have your goal before you then you can be wasting your whole life. If you are off by a little bit you will keep missing the target. You may work really hard, but it won't do you any good if you keep missing the mark.

The goal of *sīla* (morality), *samādhi* (concentration) and *paññā* (wisdom) is liberation. If they are not supporting each other you won't be working in a way that the Buddha taught us to work. Each one supports the other. Each is linked in a perfect way that helps the other. You will be working in the correct way toward a happier life when you are aiming for the correct goal.

Let's review some of the things that have been mentioned so that you keep focused on the goal. Daily sittings and moral actions should be the base of your effort. Without them you will very quickly stop making effort because you won't see the benefits accumulate in life.

Stay strong and follow these two most basic elements of the path.

Remember to avoid those people who can bring you down. They are not fun. Instead try to develop friends who are meditators and those who respect others and live a clean life. As the Buddha said, friends are the whole path. They will help to lift you up and you will do the same for them.

An internal combustion engine must have fuel, air, compression, and a spark to set off the combustion that makes the engine turn and produce power. They all must be in the correct amounts and come together at the right time. When you practice properly all the elements will come together in the correct amounts and you will produce energy and move ahead on the path. Your days and your life will be filled with joy.

When I first went to Burma and met some of Sayagyi U Ba Khin's students I realized one thing: these people were normal. They were normal in a good way, a healthy and harmonious way. There were no rough edges, and humor and smiles were a common part of their lives. I don't know of anyone who had a better sense of humor than Goenkaji. He was so fast with a quip. Many of my Dhamma friends are the same way.

The wonderful thing about this technique is that the benefits manifest themselves here and now. There is no need to wait for some afterlife to get the results of your efforts. Each step of the way brings you closer to the goal and you can feel it as it manifests in your life.

You have accomplished the most difficult part and that is finding the path and taking the first step. Now you just need to apply yourself. There is so much support available for you. May you grow in the Dhamma, may you glow in the Dhamma, and may you be truly happy.

Appendix I

Developing a Meditation Area at Home

To get the most benefit from your daily sittings it is best if you have a place to meditate that is not used for anything else. It should be such that you are not walking over it all the time or frequently disturbing it. I would like to give you examples of what other people have done in their homes to set up a separate meditation area.

One of the easiest things to do is to buy a folding screen, such as the ones they sell at World Market/Cost Plus and Pier 1. Place this in the corner of a room or at the end of the room. This affords a special space that you will only use for meditation.

A friend in Seattle had a very large living room and built a lightweight framed paper screen (shoji screen) that took up one end of the room. It even had a door. It looked very Japanese and four or five people could sit there comfortably.

A couple I know from San Diego had adjacent offices in two separate rooms in their home. They had a door built between the two rooms that they left open and one sat on either side of their little instant meditation room.

A friend in England put his meditation room in his unfinished attic. There wasn't a stairway to the attic so he would jump up on the stairway post and pull himself up into the attic through the trap door. Once up there he would carefully climb over the rafters to the corner he had built for himself. He had laid down a few sheets of plywood with carpet on top and had a nice place where four people could sit. Only recommended for the strong and nimble.

Another friend installed a drop down stairway into a small unused attic space. He finished the space with sheet rock and carpeting. He and his wife would just pull down the stairs and climb up when they wanted to sit. I've actually seen this scenario a few times.

I had an enclosed back porch that we used for our room. At first it was just demarcated with a curtain. After some years I totally remodeled it with sheet rock, new carpeting, a stained glass window and an antique door. It now provides a very cozy space.

My neighbor took a small portion of her garage and built a room. It takes up about half the space in half the garage. Now she only has room for one car, but the other half now has a nice meditation room.

Numerous people have built outdoor meditation rooms. One friend that lives near an airport built double thick walls and thick shutters over the windows. A jet could take off across the road and you wouldn't hear it in this room. Usually these type of rooms are located close to the house so there isn't a long walk when it is rainy or cold. This is the most expensive way to go, but you get what you want when you are finished.

Outdoor sheds can also be converted to meditation rooms. I have seen some beautiful remodels doing this. Usually this is done in country settings where there are lots of sheds.

When you are constructing a new home this is usually the best time to build a nice meditation room right in the house. Space in attics or areas that would otherwise be difficult to make into a full size room work very well when laying out a new home.

As you can see, a meditation space can vary quite a lot. It could be small, such as using just a corner of a room with a cushion, or larger and more elaborate, all the way up to a dedicated building where you can sit and meditate. The goal is to have an area that is used only for meditation and is somewhere in your home.

Appendix II

Recommended Dhamma Books

Books focused on Vipassana

The Art of Living by Bill Hart

Sayagyi U Ba Khin Journal (VRI)

The Clock of Vipassana has Struck, Sayagyi U Ba Khin

Discourse Summaries, S.N. Goenka

For the Benefit of Many - talks and answers to questions from Vipassana students 1983-2000 S.N. Goenka (VRI).

The Essentials of Buddha Dhamma in Meditative Practice, Sayagyi U Ba Khin

Karma and Chaos by Paul Fleischman

Basic Books on Dhamma

What the Buddha Taught, Walpola Rahula

Dhammapada, Daw Mya Tin

The Buddha's Ancient Path, Piyadassi Thera

In the Buddha's Word, An Anthology, Bhikkhu Bodhi

Inspirational Books on Dhamma

Going Forth, Sumana Samanera (A BPS Wheel Publication)

The Buddha and His Disciples, Hellmuth Hecker, Venerable Nyanaponika Thera and Bhikku Bodhi

Letters from the Dhamma Brothers, Jenny Phillips

Historical Books on the Buddha

The Life of the Buddha by Ñāṇamoli Thera – Historical and Inspirational

The Search for the Buddha, (originally published as *The Buddha and the Sahibs*), Charles Allen

The Historical Buddha by H.W. Schumann – it provides interesting historical, social context of the Buddha's life and teaching (although it doesn't discuss meditation).

Advanced Books on the Dhamma

The Udana, John Ireland

The Manuals of Dhamma, Ledi Sayadaw

Learning Pāli - Basic

The Gem Set in Gold – chanting from the ten-day course – good for learning Pāli

The Pāli Workbook – Lynn Martineau

Books for Pilgrims

Along the Path, Kory Goldberg & Michelle Décary

Middle Land Middle Way, Venerable S. Dhammika

Be sure to check out the website *www.pariyatti.org* for many jewels that they have collected and can be downloaded. The books listed above should all be available for sale there too, as well as CDs/MP3s and videos/MP4s.

Vipassana Meditation Centers

Courses of Vipassana meditation in the tradition of Sayagyi U Ba Khin as taught by S. N. Goenka are held regularly in many countries around the world.

Information, worldwide schedules and application forms are available from the Vipassana website: www.dhamma.org

ABOUT PARIYATTI

Pariyatti is dedicated to providing affordable access to authentic teachings of the Buddha about the Dhamma theory (*pariyatti*) and practice (*paṭipatti*) of Vipassana meditation. A 501(c) (3) non-profit charitable organization since 2002, Pariyatti is sustained by contributions from individuals who appreciate and want to share the incalculable value of the Dhamma teachings. We invite you to visit *www.pariyatti.org* to learn about our programs, services, and ways to support publishing and other undertakings.

Pariyatti Publishing Imprints

Vipassana Research Publications (focus on Vipassana as taught by S.N. Goenka in the tradition of Sayagyi U Ba Khin)
BPS Pariyatti Editions (selected titles from the Buddhist Publication Society, co-published by Pariyatti in the Americas)
Pariyatti Digital Editions (audio and video titles, including discourses)
Pariyatti Press (classic titles returned to print and inspirational writing by contemporary authors)

Pariyatti enriches the world by
- disseminating the words of the Buddha,
- providing sustenance for the seeker's journey,
- illuminating the meditator's path.